Words of Wisdom

―――――※―――――

Lessons Learned While Walking With God

Cindy August

Creative Books Plus publishing

ISBN: 9781970947014

Creative Books Plus Publishing

Contents

DEDICATION

I dedicate this book to my family— my sons, my grandchildren, and those who carry a piece of my heart.

To my spiritual sons and daughters, may these words remind you that God's love never gives up, never lets go, and never fails.

To the friends, mentors, and prayer warriors who encouraged me, believed in me, and stood beside me through every season—thank you. Your faithfulness mattered more than you know.

And above all, to my Lord and Savior, Jesus Christ— this book is my offering of love to You.

You are the Author of my story, the Healer of my heart, and the Teacher of every Heart Lesson I've learned.
Thank You for walking with me through brokenness and beauty, for turning my mistakes into mercy, and my tears into testimony.

May every page of this book bring You glory.
May every reader feel Your presence and hear Your voice.
Let each lesson become a light, guiding hearts closer to You.

This work is Yours, Lord. Breathe upon it with Your Spirit, and send it wherever healing is needed.
In all things, may *Your will* be done — in me, through me, and beyond me.

In Jesus' name,

Amen.

INTRODUCTION

In the spring of 2009, I kept hearing a conversation in my mind. It reminded me of the story of young Samuel—how the Lord called to him again and again until he finally recognized His voice (1 Samuel 3:4–10). It didn't take long for me to realize the Lord was speaking to me... about writing a book.

This is what I heard:

"Me? You want me to write a book? You're kidding, right?"
You're not.
Okay... once upon a time—
No, not that kind of book?
Hmm... maybe a story about Susan coming in from the rain on a—
No, not that kind either?

Okay, Lord... what is this book about? Me?

Oh... that's a very short story. I was born, I'm married, and I have two sons and two beautiful granddaughters.
There. Short. Sweet. Simple. To the point.

Details? You want details?

Lord... You know me.

Okay, so my husband and sons say I give too many details—but I'll give it a try.

I was born on October 8, 1959, at 6:00 a.m. in Scotland Memorial Hospital in Laurinburg, North Carolina. The sun was shining, and the birds were singing—

No... not *that* detailed?

Okay, Lord... so where do You want me to start?

Writing about myself has never been easy. Where do I begin? How does it end? And what about all the life that happens in between?
Do I start with the ministry You called me to before the foundation of the world?
Do I start with the day I gave my life to Jesus?
Or maybe, Lord... I should start with the wisdom You've allowed me to gain through life's experiences—so that others can learn from my mistakes as well as my victories.

That's when it became clear. This book isn't really *about* me. It's about what God does through an ordinary life that says *yes*.

Words of Wisdom was first written for my granddaughters. But it soon became evident that it was meant for anyone who would open these pages—anyone desiring encouragement, healing, truth, and a deeper relationship with God our Father and our Lord Jesus Christ.

These are lessons written on the heart—learned through love, loss, obedience, worship, waiting, forgiveness, trust, and grace. Lessons guided by the Holy Spirit and shaped by God's unfailing love.

So, grab your favorite drink, a snack, and get comfortable.
I want to talk with you—from my heart to yours—as if we're sitting together in the same room.

May these pages remind you that God still speaks... still calls... still gently asks:

"Would you trust Me with this?"

Blessings to you always,
Cindy August

PREFACE

———— ❖ ————

I first wrote this book for my oldest granddaughter, Madison, when she was fourteen years old in 2014. I felt led to pour into her heart the wisdom, lessons, and love the Lord had taught me through life.

As time went on, I realized that other girls and women could benefit from these words as well. That's when the book's focus expanded—from *Words of Wisdom to My Granddaughters* to *Words of Wisdom to My Spiritual Daughters*.

Then something unexpected happened.
Men began reading the book too.

That's when I knew God was still shaping this work. These lessons were not meant for one generation, one gender, or one season—they were meant for anyone willing to open their heart and listen.

That's how Lessons Learned While Walking With God became the theme of this book. Every chapter was written with *you* in mind—the one holding these pages, wherever you are in your walk with God.

My prayer is that this book will encourage you, strengthen you, and gently draw you closer to Jesus—helping you see just how deeply God the Father, the Son, and the Holy Spirit love you.

Blessings to you always,
Cindy August

ACKNOWLEDGMENTS

———❦———

WITH A GRATEFUL HEART

To my mother, Geneva Boyer — thank you for your love, your selfless acts of kindness, and your endless generosity. You have always been there for me, and your example has shaped my heart more than words can express. I love you!

To my spiritual mom, Lindy Koger — thank you for your words of wisdom and for helping me grow into the woman of God I am today. Your time, teaching, and encouragement have guided me toward the destiny God ordained for my life. Thank you for every moment of support and even those times of loving correction. I love you deeply and am forever grateful.

And to every woman of God who has poured into my life — thank you for your prayers, your encouragement, and your example. You have helped me become who I am in Christ today. I love you all!

I thank God for each of you who has touched my life with faith and love. — Inspired by Philippians 1:3

THE FEAR OF THE LORD

The Beginning of Wisdom

"The fear of the Lord is the beginning of wisdom, and the knowledge of the Holy One is understanding." Proverbs 9:10

My Story: From Fear to Freedom

When I was a young child, my grandparents often took me to church with them. I loved going. At ten years old, I received Jesus Christ as my Lord and Savior.

I still remember the preacher's sermon that day. He preached about hell — about fire, judgment, and eternal separation from God — and I'll admit, it scared me half to death. That message put the fear of God in me, but not the kind that brings awe and reverence. It was the kind of fear that made me afraid of God's anger, afraid to fail, afraid to make Him mad.

So, I served God not because I loved Him, but because I feared Him.

Back then, there were a lot of rules. I wasn't allowed to go bowling, skating, dancing, or even watch TV. I couldn't play cards or wear pants. If I did, I was told I wasn't saved. There seemed to be so many "don'ts" that I forgot the joy of what I *could* do — love God, love people, and grow in grace.

For me, life as a child was hard. I enjoyed those things I wasn't supposed to do, and it made me feel like I could never measure up.

As a little girl, I was also taught that every time I sinned, I lost my salvation — and had to ask Jesus back into my heart. Can you imagine? For five years straight, I prayed the sinner's prayer almost every day because I thought I had to "get saved" again.

By the time I was fifteen, I was exhausted and confused. I told God, *"I still believe in You, and I love You, but I just can't follow all these rules."*
So I walked away from serving Him.
I became what I call an *on-again, off-again Christian.*

Every time I sinned, I thought I was done for. I didn't understand His love, His grace, His mercy, His forgiveness, or His goodness.

Heart Lesson

Then came the day that changed everything.

On Wednesday, January 16, 1991, I was flipping through TV channels when one suddenly froze on a Christian program. No matter how much I tried to change it, it wouldn't move. Finally, I said, *"Fine! I'll just watch this!"*

The preacher on the screen said,

"There's a woman sitting in her living room chair. Are you sick and tired of being sick and tired?"

Without even thinking, I said out loud, *"Yes, I am!"*

Then he said,

"Get up right now, call my prayer partner, and give your heart back to the Lord."

So, I did. I made the call, prayed the prayer, and rededicated my life to Jesus Christ.

At that time, I was suffering from bronchitis and Chronic Fatigue Syndrome. There was no known cure — and honestly, there still isn't. But when I hung up the phone, the Holy Spirit met me in that living room. I dropped to my knees as His power came over me, and all the infection in my sinuses cleared instantly.

I felt better — not completely healed yet — but I knew God was doing something.

That Saturday, my friend Debbie invited me to church. When I walked through the doors on Sunday, January 20, 1991, I knew I was home. The presence of the Holy Spirit was so strong that I cried through the entire service.

Afterward, I spoke to the pastor and told him what I'd been taught — that every time I sinned, I had to ask Jesus into my heart again.
He smiled kindly and said,

"Cindy, when you sin, just ask the Lord to forgive you and keep walking with Him."

That moment changed everything. A heavy weight lifted off my shoulders. I understood — really understood — *grace* for the first time.

Two weeks later, while praying in the shower, I said,
"Lord, I want to be able to run, jump, shout, and praise You — and I want to be able to breathe."

As soon as I said "breathe," I took a deep breath — something I hadn't been able to do in a long time. I turned the water off, grabbed my towel, and ran up and down the stairs Praising the Lord!

That morning, God completely healed me.

From that day forward, I promised I would never again live an "on-again, off-again" Christian life. I may stumble, but I won't turn my back on Him.

He showed me His love, His grace, His mercy, His forgiveness, and His goodness — and He brought me back into His loving embrace.

I will praise Him all my days for healing both my heart and my body.

"Do not be wise in your own eyes; fear the Lord and depart from evil. It will
be health to your flesh and strength to your bones."
— Proverbs 3:7–8

Reflection & Response

The fear of the Lord isn't about punishment — it's about reverence, awe, and love.
True fear of God means knowing who He is: holy, powerful, merciful, and full of compassion.

When we understand His love, fear turns into worship. It draws us closer instead of pushing us away.

Ask yourself:

Do I serve God out of fear — or out of love?

Do I see Him as angry — or as a Father who delights in me?

Let His love cast out every false fear and replace it with peace and awe.

Heart Talk with God

Be still before Him. Let His presence replace fear with peace.

Father, help me to understand the difference between fear and reverence.

Thank You for showing me Your love and grace even when I didn't understand it.

Teach me to serve You out of love, not fear.

Remind me daily of Your mercy and patience toward me.

I praise You for healing my body and restoring my heart.

"Perfect love casts out fear — and draws you closer to the One who loves you most."

Heart Reflections

Take a quiet moment to pause and let God speak to your heart.

LOVE THE LORD

───── ❧ ─────

The Greatest Commandment

"Teacher, which is the great commandment in the law?"
Jesus said to him, "You shall love the Lord your God with all your heart,
with all your soul, and with all your mind.
This is the first and great commandment."
— Matthew 22:36–38

Loving God Above All

It is so important that we love the Lord God above everything — above ourselves, our parents, our friends, our work, our dreams, even our ministries.
Love Him more than your free time, your hobbies, your phone, or your plans.
Love Him *above everything.*

Why? Because He commands us to.
And because when you love God with all your heart, soul, mind, and — as *Mark 12:30* adds — *strength,* you'll naturally put Him first in all things. But when you don't, it's easy to drift away from the One who loves you most.

The truth is that this world is full of distractions that pull at our hearts and time.
I know — I've been there. Sometimes we get so busy with what *we* want to do that we forget to spend time with the very One who gives us life and purpose.

For me, I've learned that the best time to meet with the Lord is early in the morning, before my feet ever touch the floor.

Once I start the day, I'm running nonstop. But in those first quiet moments — before the world wakes up — it's just me and Him.

Sometimes it's ten minutes, sometimes two hours. I never notice how much time has passed when I'm in His presence.

And the most beautiful part? He knows. God knows your heart, your thoughts, and your intentions.

He knows what you're trying to say even when words don't come easily.

Scriptures to Remember

"But the Lord said to Samuel, 'Do not look at his appearance or at his physical stature, because I have refused him. For the Lord does not see as man sees; for man looks at the outward appearance, but the Lord looks at the heart.'"
— 1 Samuel 16:7

"O Lord, You have searched me and known me. You know my sitting down and my rising up; You understand my thought afar off. You comprehend my path and my lying down and are acquainted with all my ways."
— Psalm 139:1–3

"Search me, O God, and know my heart; Try me, and know my anxieties; And see if there is any wicked way in me, and lead me in the way everlasting."
— Psalm 139:23–24

Heart Lesson

There's a story in *Mark 10:20–22* that always touches me.

A rich young man came to Jesus and said he had kept all the commandments since his youth.

"Then Jesus, looking at him, loved him, and said to him,
'One thing you lack: Go your way, sell whatever you have and give to the poor, and you will have treasure in heaven; and come, take up the cross, and follow Me.' But he was sad at this word and went away sorrowful, for he had great possessions."

The young man walked away, not because he didn't love God — but because he loved other things more.

When I read this, I have to ask myself, *"Where is my heart today?"*
Is it loving and serving the Lord, or is it distracted — caught up in "modern riches" like TV, social media, games, shopping, or work?

I can't answer for anyone but myself. I've been there. I've had seasons when I wanted my way more than His.
But every time, His love and goodness led me back.

"Or do you despise the riches of His goodness, forbearance, and long-suffering, not knowing that the goodness of God leads you to repentance?"
Romans 2:4

One day, as I reread the passage in Mark 10, the Holy Spirit showed me something I had never noticed before:

"Then Jesus, looking at him, loved him, and said to him..."

Those words stopped me in my tracks — **He loved him!**

Before Jesus corrected him, before He told him to give up his riches, He looked at him *with love.*

That revelation brought tears to my eyes.
I sat there, overwhelmed, realizing — that same love is for me too.

He looks at me and loves me.
He looks at you and loves you — even when we're distracted, disobedient, or distant.

Oh, what an incredible God we serve!
Thank You, Father, for Your lovingkindness, for leading me back to You every time I wander, and for always welcoming me into Your loving embrace.

Reflection & Response

Loving God fully means giving Him our whole heart — not just the parts that are convenient or comfortable.
It means letting go of distractions, surrendering our plans, and trusting that His ways are better.

Ask yourself:

What do I give more time and attention to than God?

What's keeping me from loving Him with all my heart?

Do I truly believe that His love is greater than anything I could gain on my own?

Let the Holy Spirit show you where He's calling you back to *first love* — that pure, joyful devotion where your heart beats in rhythm with His.

Heart Talk with God

Be still before Him. Let His love quiet your heart and draw you near.

Father, teach me to love You above all else.
Reveal anything that has taken first place in my heart.
Thank You for loving me even when I fall short.
Help me to return to my first love — to delight in Your presence again.
Let my time with You be filled with joy, not obligation.

"Loving God isn't about rules — it's about relationship. When you fall in love with Him, obedience becomes joy."

Heart Reflections

Take a quiet moment to pause and let God speak to your heart.

PRAISE & WORSHIP

The Sound of a Thankful Heart

"Oh come, let us sing to the Lord!
Let us shout joyfully to the Rock of our salvation.
Let us come before His presence with thanksgiving;
Let us shout joyfully to Him with psalms.
Oh come, let us worship and bow down;
Let us kneel before the Lord our Maker."
— Psalm 95:1–2, 6

A Song from the Heart

Sing to the Lord — make a joyful noise! That's me!
I praise God because He has taught me to sing with my hands — *Signing for Worship!* What a wonderful way to express my love to Him.
Signing is my personal worship. It's how I pour out my heart through praise and song.

If I need an answer, I begin by thanking Him for the answer before it comes.
If I'm walking through a trial, I praise Him for who He is — knowing He brought me through before, and He'll do it again.

Sometimes, I'll put on a song and play it on repeat until it sinks into my spirit.
The sorrow fades, the heaviness lifts, and joy begins to flow again.

What about you?
What song helps break your sorrow?

What praise helps you shift your focus from problems to the power of God?

Here are some of mine — declarations of praise that never fail to lift my heart:

LORD, YOU are Holy and Righteous!
YOU are Glorious and Victorious!
YOU are my Strength and my Strong Tower!
YOU are my Comforter and Healer!
YOU are my Lord and Savior, my God and my King!
YOU lift my head and deliver me!
YOU are my Shepherd, my Wonderful Counselor!
YOU are my Best Friend!
YOU are Everything that I need!!

Heart Lesson

Did you know there are seven different Hebrew words for "praise"?
Each one captures a unique expression of love and worship toward God.

In my book *Signing for Worship,* I share from the beautiful study *The Priesthood of the Believer* by Dr. Sam Sasser and Dr. Judson Cornwall. These words reveal the depth of what it truly means to praise the Lord.

Here they are:

Towdah — Thanksgiving Praise

Yadah — Power Praise

Halal — Celebration Praise

Zamar — Melodious Praise

Barak — Adoration Praise

Tehillah — Singing Praise

Shabach — Shouting Praise

Let's look closer at the first three:

Towdah — *The Sacrifice of Thanksgiving*

Towdah is when we lift our hands, palms open, offering thanks for things we have not yet received — and for the things we already have.

It's praise by faith.
Have you ever not felt like praising God but did it anyway?
That's Towdah praise. It's costly — it takes everything inside you to raise your hands and whisper, *"Thank You, Lord."*
And God always responds to a sacrifice of praise.

Yadah — *The Power of Reaching Up*

Yadah also means lifting hands, but this time it's reaching outward — extending our hands in power, confession, and thanksgiving.

Yadah praise moves us from *thinking* about worship to truly *feeling* it.
This is where *Signing for Worship* begins — when your heart overflows and your body joins in to express it.

When you reach this point, standing still isn't enough.
Your hands want to move; your body wants to dance.
You can't help but express your love to God!

Halal — *The Celebration*

Halal means to celebrate, shine, boast, or be "clamorously foolish" before the Lord.
This is the kind of praise David showed when he danced before God with all his might.

That's what God invites us into — a celebration of who He is!

The Performance of Worship

Worship is deeply personal — a one-on-one act of love between you and Jesus.
Even when others are watching, true worship is intimate.

Onlookers might not understand your worship, but if your heart is pure, Jesus always accepts it.

There's no one "right" expression. Worship may come through tears, laughter, stillness, or movement — and in our case, through *signing*.

Worship is an attitude that overflows into action.
If you're lukewarm, you can't express fiery worship.
If you're bound by formality, your spirit will long to move freely.

God created us to be vocal, emotional, vibrant, and physical.
When we worship Him with all that we are — heart, voice, hands, and motion — Heaven responds.

So, I pray that the anointing of the Holy Spirit falls on you as you worship.
Be expressive!
Let your love pour out to Him without restraint.
Enter that one-on-one communication with the Lord and worship Him with freedom and joy.

We Are the Praise

"We are the praise — the song of the Lord; He sings over us."

"The Lord your God in your midst,
The Mighty One will save;
He will rejoice over you with gladness,
He will quiet you with His love,
He will rejoice over you with singing."
— Zephaniah 3:17

God Himself rejoices over you.
You are His song — His delight — His expression of love.
Your praise moves His heart.

Reflection & Response

Worship isn't about performance — it's about *presence*.
It's not about music style, sound, or stage. It's about *surrender*.

Ask yourself:

Am I worshiping to be seen — or to be with God?

Do I give God only my voice, or my whole heart?

How can I express my love for Him more freely — without fear or hesitation?

Let your life become a living song to the Lord.

Heart Talk with God

Be still before Him. Let your praise rise like incense before His throne.

Father, I thank You for the gift of worship.
Teach me to praise You in every season — in joy and in sorrow.
Fill me with boldness to worship freely and expressively.
Let my worship break chains and bring healing.
May I always remember that You delight in me — You sing over me!

"When you lift your hands in praise, Heaven leans in to listen."

Heart Reflections

Take a quiet moment to pause and let God speak to your heart.

PRAYER

Conversations That Change Everything

"In this manner, therefore, pray:
Our Father in heaven,
Hallowed be Your name.
Your kingdom come,
Your will be done
On Earth as it is in Heaven.
Give us this day our daily bread.
And forgive us our debts,
As we forgive our debtors.
And do not lead us into temptation,
But deliver us from the evil one.
For Yours is the kingdom and the power and the glory forever. Amen."
— Matthew 6:9–13

The Power of Prayer

Prayer is an essential part of your relationship with God.
I'll be honest — I was nervous in the beginning about praying, especially out loud in front of others.
But as your walk with God grows, so does your prayer life.

You'll find yourself praying or talking to God all the time.

"Rejoice always, pray without ceasing, in everything give thanks, for this is the will of God in Christ Jesus for you."
— *1 Thessalonians 5:16–18*

Prayer connects us with the One True God — a sacred oneness of Spirit where there is no division, only communion.
Through prayer, revelation flows and hearts are changed.

To be honest, my "formal" prayer life isn't always where I'd like it to be.
But my conversation with God never ends.
I talk to Him throughout the day — whether I'm whispering thanks, asking for guidance, or simply saying, *"I Love You, Lord."*

That ongoing connection is what it means to *pray without ceasing.*

I've learned to pray for others as soon as the opportunity comes.
If someone asks for prayer, I try not to wait — I pray right then, whether aloud or silently.
Because we never know what the rest of the day will bring, I've learned that obedience in prayer is often urgent and Spirit-led.

Heart Lesson

Prayer isn't about saying the right words — it's about opening your heart to the right One.

Every conversation with God shapes your spirit and deepens your trust in His love.
When you speak, He listens.
When you're silent, He still hears.

Make space today to talk to Him about everything — the little things, the big things, and the hidden things.
He longs to be part of them all.

Reflection & Response

Prayer is more than words — it's *relationship.*
It's not about getting the right phrasing or sounding eloquent; it's about being honest with God.

He already knows your heart, yet He still invites you to speak with Him.
Prayer strengthens faith, shapes your character, and opens the door for Heaven's power to move on Earth.

Don't be afraid to pray out loud or quietly in your heart.
The more you pray, the more natural it becomes.
You'll begin to notice His presence in the small things, and that awareness will change the way you see everything.

When you pray, believe that God hears you — and that He's not only listening but responding in love.

Heart Talk with God

Be still before Him. Let this be your quiet time of conversation and communion with the Lord.

Father, teach me to pray from the heart — not just with words, but with sincerity and faith.
What areas of my prayer life need to grow stronger?
When I pray for others, how can I listen more closely to Your Spirit's leading?
Help me to remember that prayer is not about performance, but about presence.
Thank You for hearing me, even when I don't have the words to say.

"When you pray, you are never alone — He is already there, waiting to listen."

Heart Reflections

Take a quiet moment to pause and let God speak to your heart.

TRUST IN THE LORD

The Beauty of Waiting Well

"Trust in the Lord with all your heart and lean not on your own understanding; in all your ways acknowledge Him, and He shall direct your paths." Proverbs 3:5–6

Trust the Lord, for He knows what is best for you. When you pray for an answer, wait for the answer. Don't do what I did—jump ahead of God when it feels like He's silent. That's what it means to lean on your own understanding. Trust me, I've been there, done that, bought the t-shirt, and now I'm writing the book on it!

"Our soul waits for the Lord; He is our help and our shield." Psalm 33:20

"Rest in the Lord and wait patiently for Him; do not fret because of him who prospers in his way." Psalm 37:7

Waiting isn't always easy, but it's always worth it. When we rush ahead, we often find ourselves in unnecessary trouble. But when we wait, God's timing always brings peace.

"I waited patiently for the Lord; He inclined to me and heard my cry." Psalm 40:1

"Those who wait on the Lord shall renew their strength; they shall mount up with wings like eagles, they shall run and not be weary, they shall walk and not faint." Isaiah 40:31

"I wait for the Lord, my soul waits, and in His word I do hope." Psalm 130:5

Heart Lesson

There are so many scriptures about waiting on the Lord—because He knows how easily we rush ahead. I can't count the times I've ignored that gentle tug of the Holy Spirit and later realized I missed a blessing that was meant for me.

Other times, when I obeyed that still, small voice, I was amazed at how perfectly things came together. Even writing this book was like that—I sensed God prompting me to start, and when I listened, everything flowed.

Sometimes it's something simple: a nudge to call a friend, visit someone who's lonely, or bless another person with something that's been sitting unused in your closet. You'll discover it was never meant for you—it was God's way of giving through you.

Trusting the Lord applies to every area of life: school, work, friendships, relationships, and marriage. He sees the full picture, while we only see a piece of the puzzle. That's why His "no" is often His protection.

Let me give you two examples of lessons learned the hard way.

Once, I wanted a new car so badly that I ignored that tug in my heart. I even prayed, "Lord, if You don't want me to have it, don't let me get it." But instead of waiting, I pushed ahead. I bought the car anyway. It was too expensive, and the payments would have forced me to take on a full-time job I didn't want. So, I returned the car—and learned that waiting would've spared me stress and regret.

Another time, I was engaged and felt that same tug not to marry. But a friend convinced me otherwise—"He's a good guy," she said. So, I went ahead. We married on Friday, and on Monday he called to say that we had to get an annulment, because his divorce hadn't gone through—he was still married to the girl in Texas! What?! Seriously?! To top it off, he had a drinking problem I hadn't known about. If only I had listened to the Holy Spirit's warning.

These experiences taught me that when we insist on having our own way, God sometimes allows it—not because it's His perfect will, but because it's His permissive will. But His perfect will always bring peace, clarity, and blessing.

So, my friend, trust the Lord and wait patiently for Him. Acknowledge Him in all you do, and He will direct your path. His way is always better, and His timing is always right.

Reflection & Response

Trust requires surrender. It means letting go of control and believing that God's plan really is for your good, even when it doesn't make sense.

He is not trying to withhold blessings from you—He's preparing your heart to handle them. Each delay, each redirection, is an invitation to lean deeper into His love and wisdom.

Ask yourself: Am I trusting His timing, or am I trying to make things happen my way?

Every time you choose to wait on Him, you're saying, "Lord, I believe You know best." And that kind of faith moves mountains.

Heart Talk with God

Be still before Him. Let this be your quiet moment of trust and surrender.

Father, teach me to wait patiently for Your perfect timing.

Help me recognize the difference between Your will and my own desires.

What area of my life am I still trying to control instead of trusting You with it?

Remind me that Your "no" is often a greater blessing than my "yes."

Strengthen my faith to follow Your leading even when I don't understand it.

Heart Reflections

Take a quiet moment to pause and let God speak to your heart.

GOD'S PLAN FOR YOU

―――――❦―――――

Trusting His Timing and Direction

*"For I know the thoughts that I think toward you," says the Lord, "thoughts
of peace and not of evil, to give you a future and a hope.
Then you will call upon Me and go and pray to Me, and I will listen to you.
And you will seek Me and find Me, when you search for Me with all your
heart. I will be found by you," says the Lord... Jeremiah 29:11–14a*

The Promise of His Plan

This has always been one of my favorite scriptures.
I remember a season when the Lord kept giving me this verse again and
again.
I'd hear it from my pastor, on the radio, in devotionals — everywhere I
turned, there it was.
And I finally realized He was speaking directly to me.

I praise God that His thoughts toward me are good.
He doesn't plan evil for me.
His desire is to give me peace, hope, and a bright future.
That's not just for me — it's for you, too!

When we pray, we can trust that He hears us.
He never says, *"I'm too busy"* or *"Come back later."*
His heart is always open.
When we seek Him sincerely, we find Him — not because we're perfect,
but because He's faithful.

If you ever hear the enemy whispering that you're not good enough, or that God isn't listening, take those thoughts captive and replace them with His truth.

"Casting down arguments and every high thing that exalts itself against the knowledge of God, bringing every thought into captivity to the obedience of Christ." 2 Corinthians 10:5

You've been washed in the blood of Jesus.
That means you can boldly enter God's presence and talk with Him freely.
Bring your needs, your worries, your dreams — and thank Him in advance for what He's already doing.

"Now this is the confidence that we have in Him, that if we ask anything according to His will, He hears us. And if we know that He hears us, whatever we ask, we know that we have the petitions that we have asked of Him." 1 John 5:14–15

Heart Lesson

God's plans are good — but sometimes they don't look the way we expect.
We may question His timing or direction, especially when we can't see the whole picture.
But His perspective is eternal; He knows the beginning and the end.

"'For My thoughts are not your thoughts, nor are your ways My ways,' says the Lord. 'For as the heavens are higher than the earth, so are My ways higher than your ways, and My thoughts than your thoughts.'"
— Isaiah 55:8–9

Like the Israelites in the wilderness, sometimes we take the long way around because of doubt or disobedience.
But even then, God doesn't abandon us — He patiently guides us back to His plan.

Maybe you're in a season of uncertainty, wondering what God is doing.
Trust Him.

Wait on Him.
His silence doesn't mean absence — it often means *preparation*.

When you stay close to Him, He'll align your steps with His perfect will.
God's greatest plan is for relationship.
He created you to walk with Him daily, to rest in His presence, and to know His love personally.
That's where true peace and purpose are found.

Reflection & Response

When we look back, it's easy to see how God was weaving things together even when we didn't understand.
He wastes nothing — not a delay, not a mistake, not even a detour.

Think of a time when you thought things were falling apart, only to realize later they were falling into place.
That's God's plan in motion.

His plan isn't just about what you *do* — it's about who you *become*.
And as you trust Him more, you'll find that His plan for your life is always better than your own.

Heart Talk with God

Quiet your heart and talk to Him. He has a plan, and it includes you.

Lord, help me to trust that Your plans are always good.
Show me the areas of my life where I've been resisting Your direction.
Teach me to listen when You speak, even when the answer is "wait."
Remind me that Your silence is not rejection — it's preparation.
Thank You for shaping my life into something beautiful according to Your purpose.

"When you can't see the plan, trust the Planner."

Heart Reflections

Take a quiet moment to pause and let God speak to your heart.

FORGIVENESS

---✦---

The Freedom to Heal

"Then Peter came to Him and said,
'Lord, how often shall my brother sin against me, and I forgive him? Up to
seven times?' Jesus said to him, 'I do not say to you, up to seven times, but up
to seventy times seven.'" Matthew 18:21–22

Learning to Forgive

This is a crucial lesson to learn. Please don't skip over this message.
I know there may be things that have happened in your life that you don't
want to forgive — but you *must*.

Forgiveness is one of the life lessons I had to learn the back in 1996.
I had a lot of unforgiveness in my heart, and over time it grew into anger
and bitterness.

That January, my dear friend and spiritual mom, Lindy, and I were on our
way to *The Fountain of Hope* to minister to the poor and homeless.
On the drive there, Lindy shared something the Lord had shown her at her
ranch about forgiveness.

She said,

"Cindy, take an ax to every tree that doesn't produce good fruit in your life,
and curse the root of bitterness!"

I looked at her and said, "What?"
She said, "Don't say *'What.'* Just do it!"

So, I did.

"I take an ax to every tree that doesn't produce good fruit in my life, and I curse the root of bitterness in my life!"

Suddenly, faces began to flood my mind — people I had held unforgiveness toward for years.

Lindy said, "Now start forgiving them! Choose to forgive them!"

So, I said, "I choose to forgive (person's name) for (the offense toward me)."

And one by one, I began to forgive them all.

That went on for about thirty minutes — the entire drive to *The Fountain of Hope*.

And I'll tell you something: **there is such freedom in forgiveness!**

Why? Because forgiveness isn't for the other person — it's for *you*.

It keeps your line of communication open with God.

Unforgiveness blocks that line.

It's one of the biggest reasons prayers go unanswered.

> *If I regard iniquity in my heart, the Lord will not hear."*
> *Psalm 66:18*

Forgiveness often comes in layers, like peeling an onion, until you get to the root.

It's not always easy, but it's worth it.

Try it now. Choose to forgive someone who hurt you. Start with the little things and work your way up to the bigger things.

I've had my share of hurt feelings and people who made me so mad I thought I'd never forgive them.

But the goodness of God changed my heart.

Sometimes my prayer was simple:

"I choose to forgive you, and may the Lord bless you."

When I pray right away, it doesn't have time to take root, grow into bitterness, or steal my peace.

But when I delay, those "instant playbacks" of hurt start to play over and over in my mind.

Isn't it time to turn off that replay and let God heal your heart?

Heart Lesson

I want you to read the rest of the parable that Jesus told about forgiveness — because it's what truly pierced my heart.

"Therefore, the kingdom of heaven is like a certain king who wanted to settle accounts with his servants. And when he had begun to settle accounts, one was brought to him who owed him ten thousand talents. But as he was not able to pay, his master commanded that he be sold, with his wife and children and all that he had, and that payment be made. The servant therefore fell down before him, saying, 'Master, have patience with me, and I will pay you all.' Then the master of that servant was moved with compassion, released him, and forgave him the debt." Matthew 18:23–27

But that same servant went out and refused to forgive someone else who owed him a much smaller debt.

When the king found out, he was furious.

"You wicked servant! I forgave you all that debt because you begged me. Should you not also have had compassion on your fellow servant, just as I had pity on you?" Matthew 18:32–33

"And his master was angry and delivered him to the torturers until he should pay all that was due to him. So My heavenly Father also will do to you if each of you, from his heart, does not forgive his brother his trespasses." Matthew 18:34–35

When I read that, it pierced my heart.

I don't want to be turned over to torment — I want to forgive!

What about you? Are you ready to forgive?

A Personal Moment of Healing

Let me share one more story before we move on.

Has Jesus Christ forgiven you? Have you received Him as your Lord and Savior? Did He wash all your sins away?

If your answer is yes, then I want you to see something with me.

Picture Jesus — beaten, hanging on the cross for you.
He died, was buried, and rose again.
Now picture Him holding you. You still have the nails and hammer in your hands — the ones that hung Him on the cross — and He's looking at you, saying,

"You're forgiven."

Now picture the person who hurt, abandoned, or betrayed you.
Place them in Jesus' arms. They're holding the same hammer and nails, and Jesus says to them too,

"You're forgiven."

If Jesus has forgiven both of you — for everything — shouldn't we also forgive one another?
Jesus says, "Yes."

"For if you forgive men their trespasses, your heavenly Father will also forgive you. But if you do not forgive men their trespasses, neither will your Father forgive your trespasses." Matthew 6:14–15

And if you haven't yet received Jesus Christ as your Lord and Savior, you can do that right now.

Prayer of Salvation

Heavenly Father,
I come to You just as I am. I know that I have sinned and fallen short, and I need Your forgiveness.

I believe that Jesus Christ is Your Son, that He died on the cross for my sins, and that He rose again so I could have new life.

Jesus, I confess You as my Lord and Savior. I ask You to forgive me, cleanse me, and make me new. I surrender my life to You and choose to follow You from this day forward.

Fill me with Your Holy Spirit. Heal my heart, renew my mind, and help me walk in Your truth and love.

Thank You for saving me. Thank You for Your grace, mercy, and eternal life.

In Jesus' mighty name,
Amen.

According to God's Word:

"Therefore, if anyone is in Christ, he is a new creation; old things have passed away; behold, all things have become new."   2 Corinthians 5:17

"If we confess our sins, He is faithful and just to forgive us our sins and to cleanse us from all unrighteousness." 1 John 1:9

"For 'whoever calls on the name of the Lord shall be saved.'" Romans 10:13

Affirmation (Read aloud):

I am forgiven. I am made new in Christ. Old things have passed away, and all things have become new. I belong to God, and nothing can separate me from His love.

Reader Response

If you prayed the Prayer of Salvation, or if you are recommitting your life to Christ, take a moment to respond below. A personal moment between you and God.

My Declaration

Today, I have made the decision to place my faith in Jesus Christ.
I receive His forgiveness, His grace, and His gift of new life.
I choose to follow Him and trust Him with my future.

Recommitment (optional)

Date: _____

Name (optional): _____

Signature (or initials): _____

This moment matters. God sees your heart, and heaven rejoices over your yes.

"Likewise, I say to you, there is joy in the presence of the angels of God over one sinner who repents." Luke 15:10

Reflection & Response

Forgiveness is a process of release — not forgetfulness, but *freedom*.
When you forgive, you're choosing peace over pain and connection over separation.

Ask yourself:

Who am I still holding in my heart?

What bitterness have I been nurturing without realizing it?

The Lord will meet you there.
Start with one name, one moment, one hurt — and let His love do the rest.
Every time you forgive, you break another chain and grow closer to the heart of Jesus.

Heart Talk with God

Be still before Him. Let Him bring to mind the people or memories that need healing.

Father, who do I still need to forgive?
Show me where bitterness may have taken root in my heart.
Give me the strength to forgive as You have forgiven me.
Teach me to walk in compassion and release the need to be right.
Thank You for setting me free through forgiveness.

"Forgiveness isn't saying what happened was okay — it's saying you won't let it hold you anymore."

Heart Reflections

Take a quiet moment to pause and let God speak to your heart.

HEALING

The Touch That Changes Everything

And Jesus went about all Galilee, teaching in their synagogues, preaching the gospel of the kingdom, and healing all kinds of sickness and all kinds of diseases among the people.   Matthew 4:23

In Chapter 1, I told you about the miraculous healing I received from Chronic Fatigue Syndrome — in the shower. That was my first personal encounter with God's healing power, a true miracle.

There are different kinds of healing. Some come instantly, others gradually. Sometimes God heals through the hands of doctors or through a process that takes time. And sometimes, He heals by calling a loved one home. But through it all, one truth remains — God is still our Healer.

Let us therefore come boldly to the throne of grace, that we may obtain mercy and find grace to help in time of need. Hebrews 4:16

When I pray for someone, I've learned to be bold — to come before God with faith and confidence. I don't pray hoping; I pray believing. I expect a miracle because I've experienced one myself.

Healing doesn't always have to take weeks or months. It can happen in a moment — in the twinkling of an eye. But sometimes, our lack of faith can hinder the work God wants to do.

And He did not do many mighty works there because of their unbelief. Matthew 13:58

Heart Lesson

One of the hardest lessons I had to learn is that not every healing comes the way we want or when we want. Sometimes healing means complete restoration here on Earth — and other times, it means going home to Heaven, where there's no more pain.

I've prayed for friends and even strangers in hospitals, only to receive a call later saying they had passed away. My heart broke each time. I called my pastor once, asking, "Why didn't God heal them?" He gently reminded me, "Cindy, He did. He healed them in His way — not yours."

That truth changed me. God is sovereign. He is merciful. He sees the whole picture. Sometimes He uses one person's passing to draw many hearts closer to Him.

I remember one pastor's story about a four-year-old boy who was desperately ill. Everyone prayed for him to live, but God called him home. At the boy's memorial service, many people gave their lives to Christ. God used that child's short life to bring salvation to others.

We may not understand God's timing, but we can always trust His purpose.

A Revelation Through My Son

When my grandfather passed away in 1991, everyone at the funeral was weeping — except my oldest son, Tom. I asked him, "Why aren't you crying?"

He said, "Because I'm jealous. Grandpa's gone home to be with Jesus. I'm still here. This world isn't my home — Heaven is."

Tom was only fourteen, and we were both new Christians. But that moment was a revelation that has stayed with me for the rest of my life.

Then in 1992, I won a cassette tape of Carman's Addicted to Jesus. The last song on it was "Third Heaven." It told the story of a man who died and described what he saw in Heaven. Then he stood before Jesus.

Jesus said, "My beloved child, there are those left behind
Who are deeply grieved at your death
They've prayed I return you to your earthly life
And because of their faithfulness to Me
I am willing to grant their request"

I said, "Lord, if my loved ones only knew
The limitless wonders of Heaven
If they could steal but one brief glimpse of glory
I know what they would do"

"Because they loved me, they'd never ask
That I return to the confines of my human body
Lord, I can't go back, please let me stay with You"

Carman's song and Tom's words changed my entire outlook on life and death. I realized that death isn't defeat — it's promotion. It's the ultimate healing.

So, when it's my time to go home, don't cry for me. Rejoice! I'll be with my Lord and Savior, singing with the hosts of Heaven:

"Holy, holy, holy, Lord God Almighty, Who was and is and is to come!"
Revelation 4:8b

"You are worthy, O Lord, To receive glory and honor and power; For You created all things, And by Your will they exist and were created."
Revelation 4:11

"Blessing and honor and glory and power, Be to Him who sits on the throne, and to the Lamb, forever and ever!" *Revelation 5:13*

Reflection & Response

Healing isn't always what we expect — but it's always what we need. Sometimes God heals the body, sometimes He heals the heart, and sometimes He heals by calling His children home.

No matter how healing comes, it's an expression of His mercy. Every answered prayer and every "not yet" is part of His plan to draw us closer to Him.

If you're praying for healing today, don't lose hope. Trust the Great Physician. Whether through medicine, miracles, or the mystery of His will, He is still healing — body, mind, and spirit.

Heart Talk with God

Be still before Him. Let Him bring peace to your body, mind, and heart. Father, teach me to trust Your plan for my healing.

Help me to believe that You are working, even when I don't see it.

Strengthen my faith to pray boldly and expect miracles.

Comfort my heart when healing doesn't look the way I hoped.

Thank You that whether in life or in Heaven, I am healed in You.

"Healing doesn't always mean staying — sometimes it means being called home to perfect peace."

Heart Reflections

Take a quiet moment to pause and let God speak to your heart.

BEHAVE LIKE A CHRISTIAN

———— ❈ ————

Reflecting Christ in Everyday Life

"Let love be without hypocrisy. Abhor what is evil. Cling to what is good."
Romans 12:9

This Scripture teaches us how to behave like a Christian. Romans 12 gives one of the clearest, most practical pictures of what it means to live out our faith daily.

But is it easy to do? Not when we try in our own strength. We can only live this way through the power of the Holy Spirit working in and through us.

When we allow His Spirit to guide our words, actions, and attitudes, we reflect the heart of Jesus to the world around us. And that's important — because we might be the only reflection of Jesus that someone ever sees.

Think about it... before you became a Christian, was there someone in your life who radiated peace, joy, kindness, or love so purely that you wanted what they had? That person's light drew you closer to Jesus — not because they were perfect, but because His presence shined through them.

That's what it means to behave like a Christian.

Heart Lesson

There's no better way to explain this life of love and humility than by letting God's Word speak for itself. Let's read the rest of Romans 12:10–21 together:

"Be kindly affectionate to one another with brotherly love, in honor giving preference to one another; not lagging in diligence, fervent in Spirit, serving the Lord; rejoicing in hope, patient in tribulation, continuing steadfastly in prayer; distributing to the needs of the saints, given to hospitality. Bless those who persecute you; bless and do not curse. Rejoice with those who rejoice, and weep with those who weep. Be of the same mind toward one another. Do not set your mind on high things, but associate with the humble. Do not be wise in your own opinion. Repay no one evil for evil. Have regard for good things in the sight of all men. If it is possible, as much as depends on you, live peaceably with all men. Beloved, do not avenge yourselves, but rather give place to wrath; for it is written, 'Vengeance is Mine, I will repay,' says the Lord. Therefore: 'If your enemy is hungry, feed him; If he is thirsty, give him a drink; For in so doing you will heap coals of fire on his head.' Do not be overcome by evil, but overcome evil with good." Romans 12:10–21

That's the picture of a Christ-like life. It's not about being perfect — it's about being willing. Willing to forgive, to serve, to be patient, and to bless even those who hurt you.

It's about letting love rule your actions, not your emotions.

When you walk in the Spirit, integrity becomes your natural response. When you let His light shine through you, He is glorified.

Let Your Light Shine

"Let your light so shine before men, that they may see your good works and glorify your Father in heaven." Matthew 5:16

Your light isn't meant to be hidden — it's meant to shine in the darkness. When people see how you respond differently — with love instead of anger, forgiveness instead of bitterness, patience instead of pride — they're seeing the reflection of Jesus.

Your life becomes the sermon. Your kindness becomes the invitation. Your peace becomes the testimony.

Reflection & Response

Living like Christ isn't about perfection — it's about connection. When we stay connected to the Holy Spirit, His fruit naturally grows in us: *Love, joy, peace, patience, kindness, goodness, faithfulness, gentleness, and self-control - Galatians 5:22–23.*

Ask yourself:

Am I living in a way that draws others to Jesus?

Do I let His love shine through me in difficult situations?

What areas of my life need more of His Spirit and less of my own effort?

Heart Talk with God

Be still before Him. Let His Spirit reveal what it means to truly walk in love.

Father, help me to love without hypocrisy.

Teach me to cling to what is good and turn from what is evil.

Fill me with Your Holy Spirit so I can live with integrity and grace.

Let my life reflect Your light in every word and action.

Make me a living testimony of Your goodness and mercy.

"When you walk in love, you preach the Gospel without saying a word."

Heart Reflection

Take a quiet moment to pause and let God speak to your heart.

ABSTINENCE

Waiting with Wisdom and Worth

"Flee sexual immorality. Every sin that a man does is outside the body, but he who commits sexual immorality sins against his own body. Or do you not know that your body is the temple of the Holy Spirit who is in you, whom you have from God, and you are not your own? For you were bought at a price; therefore glorify God in your body and in your spirit, which are God's." 1 Corinthians 6:18–20

This Is Not an Easy Subject

This is a subject many people today don't want to hear about. But please—learn from my mistakes.
Do not take the attitude that you can do whatever you want because "it's your life." It is not—at least, not anymore.

Once you receive Jesus Christ as your Lord and Savior, your life belongs to Him.

Let go and allow the Holy Spirit to lead and guide you through this life. Trust me—you will be glad you did.

"It is God's will that you should be sanctified: that you should avoid sexual immorality; that each of you should learn to control your own body in a way that is holy and honorable." 1 Thessalonians 4:3–4 (NIV)

Heart Lesson

This subject matters deeply to me because I got pregnant out of wedlock when I was seventeen years old. When the baby's father found out I was pregnant, he left.

Looking back, hindsight brings so many questions:
Why didn't I wait?
Why did I give in so easily?
Why didn't I respect myself more—and require him to respect me too?
Why was I searching for love in all the wrong places instead of accepting the love of Jesus to carry me through?

Sin may feel good for a while, but it doesn't feel good once you come to your senses. It leaves behind regret.

The devil brings condemnation, but the Holy Spirit brings conviction—and conviction is meant to lead us back to God.

Some people learn from others' mistakes; others are hard-headed and must learn for themselves. I pray you will learn from my mistakes and from those who have gone before you. Remember—there are consequences to our actions.

And let me say this clearly: I do **not** regret my sons at all. I love them with all my heart and am incredibly proud of them.
My regret is not waiting to have a husband first.

A Conversation That Broke My Heart

I was talking to a friend recently about this very subject, and their response was,
"Nobody does that anymore. Everyone wants a test drive to make sure they are the one. If not, then I'll test drive someone else."

My response was immediate—*What? Are you kidding me?*
Do you really want to be considered a "test drive"?

What if you spend years with someone who never wants to get married, while you do? What if marriage was in your heart all along—but not in theirs? Will you continue living in sin, knowing you are grieving God, simply because you don't want to walk away?

Trust me—I've been there.

Years of living in sin, hoping for a better outcome each time—insanity. Or worse, living with a man knowing exactly what kind of person he is, but marrying him anyway because I didn't want to be alone.

That marriage did not last. I was miserable, and so was he.

The Truth About Waiting

So what am I trying to tell you?

Wait.

Wait for the man or woman God has chosen for you.
Have respect for yourself—and require respect from the person who wants your heart.

They should treat you like the prince or princess God created you to be.

"Now the body is not for sexual immorality but for the Lord, and the Lord for the body." 1 Corinthians 6:13b

Remember this: you are precious to God—fearfully and wonderfully made.
And you are precious to me, too. I love you very much.

Grace for a New Beginning

If you are already having sex or living with someone outside of marriage, stop. Do no more. Come to Jesus, ask Him to forgive you, and know this truth—the slate is washed clean.

You can begin again. Fresh. New. Restored.

"...And Jesus said to her, 'Neither do I condemn you; go and sin no more.'"
John 8:11b

Please don't think I am nagging, fussing, judgmental, or out of touch. I am
not.
I am doing my very best to save you from heartache and to help you keep
your relationship with God in right standing.

The Real Consequences

Have you thought about what could happen if you—or your
girlfriend—get pregnant out of wedlock?
If you are young and still in school, how will you support yourself and
your child?

I have known young women who were kicked out of their homes and
disowned by their families. I was blessed enough to have my family—but
not everyone is.

When I was eighteen, I got engaged. He believed that since we were
engaged, sex was acceptable. I told him "No"—and I kept saying "No"...
until one day I gave in.

Not long afterwards, the relationship ended, I found out I was pregnant
again. This time my mother told me,
"You're not going to have two kids out of wedlock."

I had to marry the baby's father. The marriage lasted only six months. I
didn't love him. I didn't want to be with him. And we were both unhappy.

God's way is always better than our shortcuts.

The Lies of the World

The world says, *"It's my body; I'll do what I want."*
But God says, *"You are not your own."*

The world says, *"If I get pregnant, I'll have an abortion."*
But that is a life—a living human being created by God.

Adoption is a better choice than abortion—but why face that pain at all when obedience removes it?

And with HIV, AIDS, and countless sexually transmitted diseases today—are you willing to risk lifelong consequences for a moment of pleasure?

Please—wait.
And again, I say—**wait**.

I love you too much to stay silent.

A Closing Word of Love

Again, I am not condemning you or judging you if you've already made these choices. I simply want you to see the big picture—not just the moment you're in.

I wish someone had spoken to me this clearly—with this much love—before I learned the hard way.

If you hear anything in these words that doesn't sound like love, know this: it is not from me—it is from the enemy.

Reflection & Response

Your body is holy ground — a temple for the Holy Spirit. God calls you to purity not to restrict you, but to protect you.

Ask yourself: Have I been giving away what belongs to God?

Am I trusting Him enough to wait for His best?

Do I believe I am worth being loved in a holy, honorable way?

If you've made mistakes, His forgiveness is waiting. You can start again today.

Heart Talk with God

Be still before Him. Let His grace cover every wound, and His love make you whole.

Father, I give You my heart, my body, and my future. Forgive me for the times I've gone my own way.

Heal the places where I've been hurt or deceived.

Teach me to honor You with purity, strength, and patience.

Help me to wait for the one You have chosen for me — in Your perfect timing.

"Purity isn't about perfection — it's about direction. Every step toward God is a step away from regret."

Heart Reflection

Take a quiet moment to pause and let God speak to your heart.

MARRIAGE

A Covenant of Love and Grace

"He who finds a wife finds a good thing, and obtains favor from the Lord."
Proverbs 18:22

You must wait for the person God brings into your life. Doing so will save your heart from unnecessary pain and disappointment.

I can almost hear someone saying,

"But I love him," or "She's the one for me."

My question to you is this: Did God send them to you?

Trust me — it's better to wait for the right person than to spend years walking through heartbreak, disappointment, and court battles. I know this firsthand.

Heart Lesson

I want to share this with humility and transparency — not as a confession of failure, but as a testimony of grace. I did not always wait on God's best for my life, and I paid for those choices with heartache. But God, in His mercy, did not give up on me.

Marriage with the right person is a beautiful thing. I won't share all the heartaches from my past, but I will share the blessings of the husband God brought into my life — my husband, Don.

As of this writing, we've been married for over thirteen years, and I never knew marriage could be this good.

Does that mean we never disagree? Of course not. But we've learned that how you handle disagreement is what matters most. We talk, we listen, we forgive, and we laugh — a lot.

God knew exactly who to bring into my life and when.

The Story of Us

After several painful relationships, I decided I was done with men. I told God, "I'll just stay single." But little did I know, the one He had for me was just around the corner.

On November 11, 2011, my uncle passed away. That morning, I told the Lord,

"Life is too short. I want to enjoy my life while I wait for Your return."

That evening, I went out to a country bar to listen to a live band — one of the musicians went to my church. When Don walked off the dance floor, he saw me standing nearby, came over, and asked me to dance. We danced the rest of the night together.

The next night, I went back. He was already there, waiting. We danced again — sometimes with others, but always coming back to each other.

Later in the evening, around 11pm, Don was getting ready to leave. I asked him, "Why are you leaving so early?" He said, "Because I have church in the morning." That caught my attention.

Over the next few weeks, we kept seeing each other there. He'd save me a seat, buy me a Coke (he drank Diet Coke), and we'd dance, talk and laugh.

Then, in December, my car battery died. Don asked, "How are you going to get to the club?" I said, "I'll just find someone to jump the car." He replied, "Oh no, you won't — I'll buy you a new battery tomorrow after work."

When he came the next day, he told me,

"God told me to take care of you."

I'll be honest — I wanted to run. He was nine years older, and I thought, "Lord, this isn't what I pictured."

But God was unfolding His plan.

Soon after, some friends from church told me they'd been praying and that God told them to give me a park-model mobile home. When I accepted it, I asked Don, "Would you help me move in on Christmas Eve? I'll cook you Christmas dinner." He agreed.

After moving everything, we watched a movie and talked until 9pm and then he went home. On Christmas Day, as I prepared for him to visit, I heard the Holy Spirit whisper:

"Give him a chance."

When Don came over, we talked for seven hours straight, shared dinner, and watched a movie. At 9pm he went home. That night, I gave him my heart.

The next day, we went window shopping. While looking at jewelry, I spotted a beautiful engagement ring — he quietly put it on layaway.

On February 18, 2012, while I was at work, he surprised me. When I came home for lunch, he had lunch ready and said,

"If I got your engagement ring out of layaway, would you wear it?"

When I said yes, he pulled the box from the cabinet and asked,

"Will you marry me?"

Tears filled both our eyes. I said, "Yes, I will!" It was one of the sweetest moments of my life.

What Love Looks Like

Don blesses me everyday. He gives me attention, makes me laugh, and always considers my feelings. When he worked full-time, I'd lay out his clothes or surprise him with little things — just because. Now that he's retired and I work full-time, the roles have reversed — and he does the same for me, like making me breakfast or cooking dinner and bringing it to me while I'm busy writing this book.

He's gifted with his hands and loves projects. I have to be careful what I say, because if I mention an idea, he'll often make it happen!

One day, before going to babysit my granddaughter Gracie, I mentioned that it would be nice if the bedroom door faced the kitchen instead of the hallway. When I came home later — there it was! He'd moved the door!

That's love in action.

Listening to the Holy Spirit

If the Holy Spirit ever tells you, "This one is not for you," listen. God sees what we can't. He knows when a relationship will bless you — and when it will break you.

I wish I had listened when I was younger; it would have saved me years of heartache.

Marriage DOs and DON'Ts

DO:

Put God first in your marriage.

Be respectful and kind.

Be patient and understanding.

Laugh together — often.

Make time just for each other.

Do little things that show love.

Treat your spouse the way you want to be treated.

Ask for forgiveness.

Forgive quickly.

DON'T:

Don't nag or complain.

Don't criticize or control.

Don't insist on always having your way.

Don't spend more time with friends, your phone, or TV than with your spouse.

Don't bring up past mistakes that should be forgiven.

These are small things — but they make a big difference.

Marriage is about teamwork, tenderness, and trust. It's not perfect, but when Christ is the center, it's beautiful.

Scriptures for a Godly Marriage

"Wives, submit to your own husbands, as to the Lord. For the husband
is head of the wife, as also Christ is head of the church; and He
is the Savior of the body. Therefore, just as the church is subject
to Christ, so let the wives be to their own husbands in everything."
Ephesians 5:22–24

"Husbands, love your wives, just as Christ also loved the church and gave
Himself for her... that He might present her to Himself a glorious church,
not having spot or wrinkle... So husbands ought to love their own wives as
their own bodies." Ephesians 5:25–29

"Do not let your adornment be merely outward... but let it be the hidden person of the heart, with the incorruptible beauty of a gentle and quiet spirit, which is very precious in the sight of God."   1 Peter 3:3–5

"Who can find a virtuous wife? For her worth is far above rubies. The heart of her husband safely trusts her... She does him good and not evil all the days of her life." Proverbs 31:10–12

Heart Talk with God

Be still before Him. Let Him teach you how to love the way He loves. Father, thank You for being the author of love.

Teach me to build my marriage on You alone.

Help me to forgive quickly and love deeply.

Make me patient, kind, and thoughtful toward my spouse.

Keep us united in Spirit, purpose, and prayer.

Let our marriage reflect Your covenant love to the world.

"A God-centered marriage isn't built on perfection — it's built on forgiveness, laughter, and two hearts that never stop choosing each other."

Heart Reflection

Take a quiet moment to pause and let God speak to your heart.

THE DARKEST TIMES IN MY LIFE

From Brokenness to Breakthrough

"The Lord is near to those who have a broken heart, and saves such as have a contrite spirit." *Psalm 34:18*

I told you back in the chapter on *Marriage*, "I won't share all the heartaches from my past."
But as I prayed, I felt the Holy Spirit urging me to write this chapter.
I wasn't planning to—but I couldn't shake the feeling that someone needed to hear this.
So here it is... my story of how God met me in the darkest times of my life.

When Everything Fell Apart

In 1986, my husband came home at 2:30 a.m. from a date and told me our marriage was over.
The pain was unbearable. I was a believer in Jesus Christ, but I wasn't serving Him at the time.
I couldn't function. I cried all the time—at home, and sometimes even at work when no one was looking.

Eventually, I pulled myself together, but instead of healing, I went searching for love in all the wrong places.
I partied every weekend, I loved to dance, and though I wasn't much of a drinker, I tried to look like I was having fun.
But deep down, I was broken and lost.

I remember sitting on my bed one night, surrounded by bills I couldn't pay. I must have whispered a prayer, because suddenly I stopped crying. A peace came over me—a calm I couldn't explain.

And I realized later... **Jesus hears our prayers, no matter how small.**

A Storm I Didn't Expect

In 1989, I remarried. Then, in 2007, my husband was arrested and sent to jail.
The shock and pain crushed me. I cried until there were no tears left.

Praise God that this time, I had Him to hold onto.
I clung to my Heavenly Father with everything in me.

When my pastors told me they couldn't support me financially, I found a job at Walmart.
But I was so heartbroken that some days, I couldn't even make it to work.

One day, the Holy Spirit whispered to my heart:
"Put on *Praise You in This Storm* by Casting Crowns."

So I did.
The first day, I played it for three hours—crying until I had no more tears.
The second day, I played it for one hour.
The third day, just thirty minutes.
Each time, the tears came... and then peace.

That song became my anthem whenever life felt like it was falling apart.
Through worship, my heart found healing again.

Heart Lesson: Trusting God in the Valley

During that season, I had to depend on the Lord for everything.
I worked as a courier, spending long hours alone in the car—just me and God.
I talked to Him constantly. Those were sacred hours of worship and

communion that drew me closer to Jesus, my Heavenly Father, and the Holy Spirit.

Then came another test. The company I worked for shut down. I lost my job—and the company car that went with it.

A friend from church told me the Lord had spoken to her to buy me a car. She bought a used van, put on new tires, a new battery, paid six months of insurance, and had it detailed.
I was overwhelmed with gratitude.

God always provides.

I later worked one day a week at a Christian bookstore. My paycheck for two weeks was $74.
When I couldn't afford rent, a couple from church let me live with them to help care for their newborn. I lived with them for about a month or two.

Then, a lady from church offered me a place to stay and a job as her secretary—but when I arrived, she didn't answer the door.

Everything I owned was packed in my van. So that night, I slept there.
I told myself, "I can do this. I used to live in my truck as a driver—this isn't new."

I didn't realize then that God was preparing me for the next breakthrough.

Provision in the Wilderness

My boss at the Christian bookstore found out about my situation and offered me the back of the store to stay in.
She said, "You'll have a bed, a bathroom, and a kitchen."

I stayed there for two weeks—until my son found out and insisted I move in with him.
When that didn't last, I went back to my van again.

A church friend later invited me to live with her and help care for her husband, who had open-heart surgery.
I stayed for nine months, until he passed away, and then she asked me to leave.

Homeless again.

I moved in with a pastor's family for a short time, then with my son again. Eventually, I found a temporary job in Tucson helping a friend recover from surgery—but it ended after two months.

Then came another open door. A dear friend named Miss Lou told me about a job opening at her company.
I went on Monday for an interview, and I got the job!

It came with my own home—utilities included. That was September 1, 2010. **That was the turning point.**

Breakthrough and New Beginnings

Even during all that time, I continued visiting my husband in prison.
But on January 9, 2011, something shifted.

That day, I wore my hair fixed up and a black dress with flowers.
My husband told me, "Don't wear your hair like that again until I get out," and criticized what I was wearing.
I excused myself, went to the restroom, and cried.

For months, he'd argued that "Jesus wasn't enough" and that "animal sacrifices were still required."
That day, I'd had enough. I prayed, *"Father, please release me from this marriage."*

That night, I dreamed of freedom.
When I told my pastor, he said, "No condemnation. Go get your divorce."

In June 2011, I was divorced.
Five months later, in November, I met Don.
We married in June 2012—and God has truly blessed our marriage.

As I write this, it has been fourteen years since the day Don and I first met on November 11, 2011. We have now been married for over thirteen years. My heart overflows with gratitude for how far the Lord has brought me — from brokenness to breakthrough, from tears to triumph.

Heart Reflection

Life isn't always easy. But even when everything falls apart, **God is faithful**.

If I could do it all over again, I would never walk away from Him at fifteen. I wouldn't trade His love for anything this world could offer.

When I didn't serve Jesus, my life was chaos.
When I did, even the hard times had purpose.

So stay close to the Father, Son, and Holy Spirit.
Even when things don't go as planned—don't walk away.
Hold tight to Him through every storm.

Heart Talk with God

Be still before Him. Let His peace heal the places still tender from the past.

Father, thank You for walking with me through every dark valley.
Thank You for turning my pain into purpose and my trials into testimonies.
Help me to trust You in every circumstance—
to praise You in every storm, and to remember that You are faithful, even when life feels uncertain.

Teach me to depend on You fully and to see Your goodness in every season.
In Jesus' name, Amen.

"Even when the night feels endless, dawn always comes— and with it, the light of His love."

Heart Reflections

Take a quiet moment to pause and let God speak to your heart.

FINANCES

―――――― ❦ ――――――

Trusting God as Your Provider

"Give, and it will be given to you: good measure, pressed down, shaken
together, and running over will be put into your bosom.
For with the same measure that you use, it will be measured back to you."
Luke 6:38

More Than Money

This scripture doesn't apply only to money — it applies to everything you
give.
If you give clothes, you'll receive clothes.
If you give help, you'll receive help.
If you give love, you'll receive love.

Whatever you sow, you will also reap.

But let me be honest — the subject of finances wasn't an easy lesson for me
to learn.
I had to walk through a lot of mistakes before I understood what true
financial peace looked like.

Heart Lesson: Wisdom Over Want

The most important lesson I learned is this:
Don't go into debt.

Don't buy something you can't afford to pay for in cash.
If you can't buy it without borrowing, wait — because if you rush ahead, the blessing can quickly become a burden.

It's better to drive an old car that's paid for than a new one that steals your peace every month.

Even if you can only save $10 a month, start there.
It's not about how much you save — it's about building the *habit* of wisdom.

Trust me, one day you'll thank yourself when an unexpected expense comes up — like a flat tire, a broken refrigerator, or a medical bill — and you have money set aside.

Learning from Experience

In my earlier marriages, money seemed to disappear faster than it came in. Bills were often paid last — if at all — and that led to stress, arguments, and fear.

But in my marriage with Don, we learned to put things in proper order.

First, we pay our bills. Then, we would buy groceries.

Then, we decide if there's enough left for clothes, home projects, or personal things like nails or hair appointments (which, by the way, I now include in my monthly budget!).

It's amazing how much peace comes from *order*.

When you invite God into your finances, He brings balance.
You begin to see money as a tool, not a trap — as a blessing to manage, not a master to serve.

Practical Wisdom

Here are a few principles I've learned along the way:

Tithe faithfully.
God doesn't need your money — but He blesses obedience.
When you give Him the first 10%, He blesses the 90% far beyond what you can imagine.

"Bring all the tithes into the storehouse... and try Me now in this," says the Lord of hosts,
"If I will not open for you the windows of heaven and pour out for you such blessing
that there will not be room enough to receive it." Malachi 3:10

Avoid impulse spending.
Ask yourself before each purchase, *"Do I need this, or do I just want it right now?"*
A few moments of prayer can save years of regret.

Plan for the future.
Write down your bills, debts, and goals.
Ask God to help you be a faithful steward.
He'll give you wisdom and creativity — He might even open doors for extra income in ways you didn't expect.

Live within your means.
Be content with what you have while you work toward what you want.
Gratitude makes little feel like plenty.

Give generously.
Whether it's money, time, or kindness — giving always multiplies.
You can't outgive God. When you bless others, He blesses you.

My Turning Point

There was a time when I didn't understand how tithing and giving worked. I thought, *"How can I give when I can barely make ends meet?"*

But when I finally obeyed — even when it didn't make sense — everything started to change.

No, money didn't fall from the sky.
But somehow, God made my little go further.
Groceries lasted longer.
Unexpected discounts appeared.
People blessed me out of nowhere.

I realized that giving isn't about losing money — it's about **trusting God's provision.**

True Treasure

"But lay up for yourselves treasures in heaven,
where neither moth nor rust destroys and where thieves do not break in and steal.
For where your treasure is, there your heart will be also." Matthew 6:20–21

The truth is, your bank account doesn't measure your worth — your heart does.
God's definition of wealth isn't how much you have in the bank,
but how much peace, generosity, and contentment you have in your heart.

When you give to others, you're storing treasure in Heaven — treasure that lasts forever.

Simple Steps Toward Financial Freedom

Pray before every major purchase.

Track your income and expenses monthly.

Create an emergency fund — even a small one.

Avoid comparing your life to others.

Practice generosity, not guilt.

Seek godly counsel about money — Christian finance books, pastors, or mentors can help you build a plan rooted in wisdom.

Heart Talk with God

Be still before Him. Invite the Holy Spirit to guide every financial decision.

Father, thank You for being my Provider.
Help me to manage what You've given me with wisdom and integrity.
Teach me contentment in every circumstance.
Show me ways to bless others as You've blessed me.
Help me trust that You will always meet my needs.
I give You control over my finances — and my future.

"When you honor God with your finances, He doesn't just fill your wallet — He fills your life with peace."

Heart Reflections

Take a quiet moment to pause and let God speak to your heart.

FRIENDS

———⚜———

Choosing Wisely and Loving Deeply

"The righteous should choose his friends carefully,
For the way of the wicked leads them astray."
— *Proverbs 12:26*

The Power and Pain of Friendship

This is such a wise truth — and one I've learned the hard way!
I've had friends I thought would be there for life, only to discover they
weren't really friends at all.

Friends can be a tremendous blessing — or a stumbling block.
That's why the Bible warns us to choose carefully.
The people we spend time with can draw us closer to God or slowly pull
us away from Him.

If your faith isn't strong, even good intentions can't keep you from being
influenced by the wrong crowd.
Choose friends who build your faith — not break it down.

Heart Lesson: Guarding the Gift of Trust

As you know by now, I'm an open book. My parents used to call me
"a walking encyclopedia — you tell everything you know!" They weren't
wrong.

The good part about being open is that the devil can't use your past against you when you've already shared your story.
The downside, though, is that **not everyone deserves access to your heart.**

Be careful who you share your secrets and struggles with.
Some people may act like friends but carry hidden agendas or gossip behind your back.
I've experienced that heartbreak — people who betrayed my trust or used my vulnerability against me.

But thank God, I've also been blessed with true friends — women I can call when I need prayer, laughter, or a listening ear.
We've shared tears, coffee, and car rides full of praise music.
Those are my *"iron sharpens iron"* friends — the ones who lift me up, not tear me down.

"As iron sharpens iron, So a man sharpens the countenance of his friend."
Proverbs 27:17

Friendships in Seasons

Over the years, I've learned that not every friend is meant to stay forever.

Some friends are **for a season.**
They come into your life at just the right time, teach you something, and then move on. That's okay — they were part of your journey.

Some are **for a reason.**
Maybe they helped you through a hard time, or maybe you helped them find their way back to God.

And a few — a precious few — are **for a lifetime.**
These are your *spirit-connected* friends — the ones who know your heart, who pray for you without being asked, and who love you enough to tell you the truth in love.

Jesus: The Closest Friend of All

Then there's Jesus — the Friend who will never leave or betray you.
When I have something too personal to share with anyone else, I talk to
Him.
He listens with compassion, not judgment.
He knows my thoughts, my worries, my joys, and my tears.

> *"A man who has friends must himself be friendly,*
> *But there is a Friend who sticks closer than a brother."*
> *Proverbs 18:24*

He truly sticks closer than a brother — always near, always faithful, always
loving.
When everyone else walks away, **Jesus stays.**
When others don't understand, **He does.**

> *"Be strong and of good courage, do not fear nor be afraid of them; for the*
> *Lord your God, He is the One who goes with you.*
> *He will not leave you nor forsake you."*
> *— Deuteronomy 31:6*

That's the kind of Friend we all need — one who will never leave our side,
no matter what we've done or where we've been.

Friendship Reflection

Think about the friends in your life today:

Do they draw you closer to Jesus, or distract you from Him?

Do they encourage your walk, or drain your joy?

Are you being the kind of friend you want to have?

If there's someone who keeps pulling you into gossip, negativity, or
compromise, ask God for courage to step back.
And if there's someone who strengthens your faith, hold on to them and
thank God for them.

Remember: **friendship is a two-way blessing.**
Be the kind of friend who listens, prays, forgives, and uplifts.

Heart Talk with God

*Be still before Him. Ask Him to show you who belongs in your inner circle —
and who doesn't.*

Father, thank You for the gift of friendship.
Teach me to choose my friends wisely and to be a godly influence.
Help me forgive those who have hurt or betrayed me.
Surround me with people who love You and strengthen my faith.
Make me the kind of friend who reflects Your love to others.
And thank You, Jesus, for being my truest and closest Friend.

*"When Jesus is your best friend, you'll never feel alone —
because His love fills every space others leave empty."*

Heart Reflections

Take a quiet moment to pause and let God speak to your heart.

SONS AND SPIRITUAL SONS

Walking in Strength and Grace

A Word to My Sons and Spiritual Sons

"My son, hear the instruction of your father, and do not forsake the law of your mother; for they will be graceful ornaments on your head, and chains about your neck." Proverbs 1:8–9

A Mother's Heart

This section I dedicate to my sons, my spiritual sons, my future grandsons-in-law, and every man who reads these words.

Sons, please know that I love you wholeheartedly. You have always been in my thoughts and in my prayers. I've asked the Lord to help you become everything He created you to be — **strong in faith, steady in spirit, and steadfast in love.**

One thing I must tell you: **take care of my granddaughters — your sisters in Christ and future wives.**
Treat them as the precious jewels they are, with gentleness and honor. Respect them, protect them, and cherish them — but don't spoil them to the point of ruin. *(Smile.)*

I pray that you will walk in righteousness and live a life holy and pleasing to God so that your prayers will be heard and answered.
I pray that you will lead your families with integrity, humility, and love.

As you grow closer to the Lord, may your wife and children see Christ in you — in your words, your actions, and your heart.
May your home be a place of peace, strength, and laughter.

To my future grandsons-in-law — my prayer for you is the same.
Love my granddaughters well. Treasure them. Be her covering, her encourager, her partner in every season.
God has blessed you with her, and through that love, He will bless you both.

May the Lord prosper you in all you set your hands to do.
May your work be fruitful, your words be kind, and your heart be strong in the Lord.

"Husbands, love your wives, just as Christ also loved the church and gave Himself for her... So husbands ought to love their own wives as their own bodies; he who loves his wife loves himself." Ephesians 5:25, 28

"Husbands, likewise, dwell with them with understanding, giving honor to the wife, as to the weaker vessel, and as being heirs together of the grace of life, that your prayers may not be hindered." 1 Peter 3:7

Heart Lesson

A godly man is not measured by how strong he appears,
but by how **surrendered** he is to God's voice.

Strength is not control — it's compassion.
Leadership is not dominance — it's devotion.

When you walk in obedience to God, you become the kind of man who leads with love, listens with wisdom, and serves with humility.
Your strength becomes a shield for others, and your gentleness becomes their peace.

"Now may the God of peace who brought up our Lord Jesus from the dead, that great Shepherd of the sheep, through the blood of the everlasting covenant, make you complete in every good work to do His will."   *Hebrews 13:20–21*

A Personal Moment

When I look at the men God has placed in my life — my sons, my spiritual sons, and the godly men who have stood firm in faith —
I see the fingerprints of God's goodness.

Each of you carries something unique:
a calling, a story, a purpose that only you can fulfill.

You are warriors of faith, protectors of hearts, and reflections of the Father's love in a world that desperately needs it.

Never forget: **you were made in His image.**
Walk worthy of that calling.
The world needs men who are bold in love and steadfast in truth — men who lead with kindness and courage.

Reflection & Response

Take a quiet moment today to reflect.

How are you leading the people entrusted to you?

Are your words and actions drawing others closer to Christ?

How can you honor and cherish the people God has placed in your life —
your wife, your children, your friends, your brothers in faith?

Write what comes to mind.
Let the Holy Spirit speak to your heart about the kind of man He is shaping you to be.

Heart Talk with God

Be still before Him. Let His voice remind you that your strength begins in surrender.

Father, thank You for the men You've placed in my life — sons, fathers, husbands, and brothers in faith.
Teach me what it means to walk in righteousness, humility, and love.
Help me to lead with wisdom, serve with compassion, and honor those You've entrusted to me.
Make me a man after Your own heart — faithful, steadfast, and true. In Jesus' name, Amen.

"A man of God leads with love, protects with prayer, and shines with humility."

Heart Reflections

Take a quiet moment to pause and let God speak to your heart.

SUCCESS

---❦---

Walking in God's Purpose

"Commit your works to the Lord, and your thoughts will be established."
Proverbs 16:3

Redefining Success

When I think about success, I don't think first of money, fame, or accomplishment.
I think about **obedience**.

True success begins when Jesus becomes the Lord of your life and the Holy Spirit becomes your guide.

Through prayer, reading your Bible, and staying close to Jesus, you will find that He never leaves nor forsakes you.

Success is not found in how high you climb, but in how deeply you walk with God.

Learn from my mistakes and the mistakes of others.
Don't smoke, don't drink, don't do drugs, and don't let the world convince you that sin is freedom.
It's not. Real freedom is found only in Jesus Christ.

Have fun in life, too! Laugh a lot.
Find balance between being serious and simply enjoying the beauty of God's creation.
Set goals for your life and ask the Lord to direct your paths.

Heart Lesson: Dreams and Divine Design

When I was twelve years old, my teacher gave the class an assignment:

"Write down the goals you want to achieve in your lifetime."

I wrote things like:

Get married.

Have two sons.

Be a stay-at-home mom.

Learn sign language and teach it.

Be a radio announcer.

Race cars.

Fly an airplane.

Drive an 18-wheeler.

Go skydiving.

Those dreams seemed impossible back then — but God has a way of taking our childlike hopes and shaping them into His divine plan.

Over the next few decades, I watched Him check them off one by one.

By the time I was thirty-six, I had accomplished every one of those goals except two: driving an 18-wheeler and skydiving.
By thirty-seven, I was behind the wheel of an 18-wheeler, and at forty-four, I finally jumped out of that airplane!

And when all of those dreams were fulfilled, God whispered,

"It's time for new ones."

That's when *Signing for Worship* came about, and now *Words of Wisdom* — the journey of becoming an author and sharing His love with you.

A Personal Moment

I've learned that success is not about checking boxes — it's about walking with purpose.
It's not about being seen by the world but being known by God.

Some of my greatest "successes" have come from moments of surrender —
when I gave up my way for His,
when I stopped striving and simply trusted His timing.

There's peace in knowing that every dream, every delay, and every detour is part of His plan.

So if you're waiting on your breakthrough, don't lose heart.
Keep walking. Keep believing. Keep listening.

Because God's timing is never late — it's perfect.

Reflection & Response

Take a moment to write down the dreams that God has placed in your heart.

What are the desires that keep returning when you pray?

Are your goals aligned with His Word and His purpose for your life?

What step of obedience is God asking you to take right now?

Remember — your dreams are safest in His hands.
He knows exactly when to bring them to pass.

Heart Talk with God

Be still and let Him remind you that success begins with surrender.

Father, thank You for every dream You've placed within me.
Help me to pursue success that honors You — not success that feeds my pride.

Teach me to walk in Your timing, to work with diligence, and to rest in Your peace.

When I am tempted to compare myself to others, remind me that You have written my story with love and purpose.

May my success always reflect Your glory.

In Jesus' name, Amen.

"Success is not what you achieve — it's who you become while walking with God."

Heart Reflections

Take a quiet moment to pause and let God speak to your heart.

A NOTE FROM CINDY

—————— ⚜ ——————

From My Heart to Yours

As I wrote *Words of Wisdom: Lessons Learned While Walking With God,* I began to realize something unexpected — God wasn't only giving me words to share with others. He was gently speaking to my own heart, too.

Each chapter became a personal conversation between me and the Father — reminders of His love, His patience, and His faithfulness in every season of life. There were moments when I found myself laughing, crying, and repenting — and then resting in His peace.

This book became more than a project; it became a journey. A journey of rediscovering how deeply God loves us and how tenderly He teaches us. I pray that as you've read these pages, you've heard His still, small voice speaking to you as well — comforting you, correcting you, and calling you closer to Him.

Thank you for allowing me to share these *Words of Wisdom* with you. May they continue to inspire, encourage, and remind you that the Lord is always near — guiding your steps, growing your faith, and writing His love across your heart.

With all my love,

Cindy August

CLOSING BLESSING

My prayer for you, dear reader, is that these *Words of Wisdom* will stay with you long after you close this book. I pray that every word has drawn you closer to the Lord — that you've heard His whisper in your heart, felt His presence in your quiet moments, and found peace in knowing that He truly loves you.

May you continue to walk in His light with confidence, knowing that His hand is guiding your every step. When life feels uncertain, remember that God has already gone before you. When you feel weary, lean into His strength. And when you experience victory, give Him all the glory.

May His joy fill your mornings, His peace cover your nights, and His Word be the foundation of everything you do. Never stop learning from His lessons — they are written in love, designed to shape you, strengthen you, and remind you that you are never alone.

I bless you with wisdom to see His plan, courage to walk in His will, and faith to believe even when you can't see the way forward. You are deeply loved, divinely purposed, and eternally held in the arms of your Heavenly Father.

May your life shine with the beauty of His grace, and may every heartbeat echo the truth that God's love never fails.

With love and blessings always,

Cindy August

FINAL BLESSING

―――――⊰❦⊱―――――

"May the Lord bless you and keep you; May the Lord make His face shine upon you and be gracious to you;
May the Lord lift up His countenance upon you, and give you peace."
Numbers 6:24–26

You've reached the end of *Words of Wisdom* — but not the end of your journey.
Each page was a step, each reflection a seed planted in faith.

May you walk boldly into your next season, knowing that God's hand is on your life, His Word is your foundation, and His love is your everlasting success.

With love and blessings,
Cindy August

ABOUT THE AUTHOR

———✦———

Cindy August is an Author, Guest Speaker, Teacher, and Minister of the Gospel of Jesus Christ through songs expressed in Sign Language and flags.

She is the founder of Creative Books Plus Publishing and a faith-based writer devoted to helping others grow in their walk with God through inspiration, creativity, and grace.

Cindy is the author of *Signing for Worship, My Life Story for My Grandchild: A Fill-In Journal,* and numerous devotional and low-content books that encourage reflection and spiritual growth.

She also co-authored two works with her dad, George E. Boyer — *Flight of the Flyaways and Kold Stanton Kourage.*

Cindy and her husband, Don, live in North Carolina, and together they have two sons, two daughters, thirteen grandchildren, and five great-grandchildren.

www.ingramcontent.com/pod-product-compliance
Lightning Source LLC
Chambersburg PA
CBHW071149090426
42736CB00012B/2277